CONTEMPLATIONS ON CHARACTER

Contemplations on Character: A Guide to the Fullness of Godly Character

Copyright © 2020 Brian Guerin

All rights reserved. No part of this book may be used or reproduced by any means, graphic, electronic, mechanical, including photocopying, recording, taping, or by any information storage retrieval system without the written permission of the author except in the case of brief quotations embodied in critical articles and reviews.

Scripture taken from the New King James Version®. Copyright © 1982 by Thomas Nelson. Used by permission. All rights reserved.

Scripture quotations marked (NIV) are taken from the Holy Bible, New International Version®, NIV®. Copyright © 1973, 1978, 1984, 2011 by Biblica, Inc.™ Used by permission of Zondervan. All rights reserved worldwide. www.zondervan.com The "NIV" and "New International Version" are trademarks registered in the United States Patent and Trademark Office by Biblica, Inc.™

Scripture quotations marked (NLT) are taken from the Holy Bible, New Living Translation, copyright ©1996, 2004, 2015 by Tyndale House Foundation. Used by permission of Tyndale House Publishers, Inc., Carol Stream, Illinois 60188. All rights reserved.

ISBN: 9798642028384

*Cover design, typeset, & development by *Tall Pine Books*

|| Printed in the United States of America

CONTEMPLATIONS ON CHARACTER

A Guide into the Fullness of Godly Character

BRIAN GUERIN

BridalGlory.com

Contents

Part 1
THE BLUEPRINTS OF CHARACTER
1. A CASE FOR CHARACTER	3
2. INFRASTRUCTURE	5
3. CHOICES AND FEELINGS	11

Part 2
THE CONCRETE OF CHARACTER
4. DID YOU LEARN TO LOVE?	17
5. LOVE, THE BIBLE WAY	23
6. LOVE IS PATIENT	29
7. LOVE IS KIND	33
8. LOVE IS NOT ENVIOUS	35
9. LOVE IS NOT ARROGANT	37
10. LOVE IS NOT PROUD	39
11. LOVE IS NOT RUDE	41
12. LOVE IS NOT SELFISH	43
13. LOVE IS NOT IRRITABLE	47
14. LOVE KEEPS NO RECORD OF WRONG	51
15. LOVE DOES NOT DELIGHT IN EVIL	55
16. LOVE REJOICES IN TRUTH	57
17. LOVE PROTECTS	61
18. LOVE BELIEVES ALL THINGS	63
19. LOVE HOPES ALL THINGS	65
20. LOVE ENDURES ALL THINGS AND LOVE PERSEVERES	67

Part 3
THE PILLARS OF CHARACTER
21. THE POWER OF PURITY	71
22. A CULTURE OF HONOR	75

23. THE HUMBLE HEART	79
24. EXUDING EXCELLENCE	83
25. FOREVER FAITHFUL	89
26. INTERNAL INTEGRITY	93
27. CONCLUSIVE THOUGHTS	97
PRAYER FOR CHARACTER	99
ABOUT THE AUTHOR	101
FREE EXCERPT FROM ANGELIC HOSTS	105

PART 1
THE BLUEPRINTS OF CHARACTER

1
A CASE FOR CHARACTER

IF YOU'VE ATTENDED our schools, read our books or followed our ministry, it won't take you long to realize that we love the supernatural, the anointing and the gifts of the Spirit. Having said that, we are called to exemplify the person of Jesus Christ in *every* facet of His nature, leaving nothing out.

As a result, the topic of godly character cannot be omitted from our ministries. When you look at the dark spiral of society we are seeing a need for purity and a "called out" godliness like never before. I pray that through this work we see massive differences in our individual lives, our ministries, our marriages, and our personas as a whole.

When tackling the topic of character, I've heard things like, "Character? That's not a topic many will be drawn to." Yet we ought to be drawn to *all things Jesus*...and the topic of character is at the center of Christ's heart. Anointing, gifting, and knowledge of the Word cannot supplant character nor is an emphasis on character to eliminate the supernatural. You'll actually discover that godly character is indeed *supernatural*. Walking in integrity is just as supernatural as prophesying. Putting the grocery basket back where you found it can be just as godly as laying hands on the sick.

Throughout this book I will be bringing to light several areas of God's character and we will unpack the implications of that character in our own lives. It should go without saying but as we do, it's by no means meant to be condemning or judgmental. Perhaps you have failed in some of these areas of character. I can tell you I've failed in all of these areas. Teaching on character is by no means driven by guilt, condemnation or shame, but instead is intended to stir us up and encourage us to take on God's attributes more and more each day.

I pray that through this book you are brought into new measures and revelations of the rock-solid character of God and as a result, let His character become one with yours. As you grow in His nature and likeness, may you be well prepared to steward all that He would have for you today, tomorrow, and forever.

2

INFRASTRUCTURE

Character (noun): the mental and moral makeup of an individual.

THE ULTIMATE GOAL of life is to know God and, from that place, to reflect His likeness. Yet we are incapable of exuding a character and a moral standard that we ourselves have not been exposed to. Throughout the scripture we see the value of seeking Jesus and catching a revelation of who He is, that we might reflect His very nature. I believe in the simplicity of the gospel. I truly believe that by simply yielding to Jesus, everything else will fall into place. You can spend some time in the privacy of a prayer closet and be molded into the image of Jesus far more than reading countless self-help guides.

Yet at the same time, we see that examples of God's nature can also be found in *people*. Not only can it be *found* in people, but it can be *honored* and *duplicated* by us. In fact,

Paul made some incredible statements about character and imitation in his letters to the Corinthians.

> "Imitate me, just as I also imitate Christ." (1 Corinthians 11:1)

> "Therefore I urge you, imitate me. For this reason I have sent Timothy to you, who is my beloved and faithful son in the Lord, who will remind you of my ways in Christ, as I teach everywhere in every church." (1 Corinthians 4:16-17).

With the risk of sounding arrogant, Paul implores the church to follow him. Why? Because he knew that he was pulling from the character of God and if they looked to that example, a trickle down effect would manifest. Notice, Paul said, "My son in the faith, Timothy, will remind you of my *ways*." What are Paul's "ways"? His character. He had so allowed God's character to superimpose his, that he was comfortable putting himself out there as a tangible model for what godliness would look like in the church. To the Ephesians he expressed similar sentiments:

> "Therefore be imitators of God as dear children. And walk in love, as Christ also has loved us and given Himself for us, an offering and a sacrifice to God for a sweet-smelling aroma." (Ephesians 5:1-2)

The Greek definition of *imitate* here means to mimic, emulate, mirror, echo or reproduce. I find it interesting that he told the church to imitate God. In other words, it's a conscious choice to begin shaping your ways to match God's.

"We shall be like Him, for we shall see Him as He is." (1 John 3:2)

Of course this passage will take place at Christ's return but there is also a prophetic blueprint showing us how Christlikeness occurs—by and through beholding Him. In doing so, His temperament, personality, way of speaking, and way of responding is automatically adopted by us. This can be a long process or a slow process of development but I do believe these things can be accelerated through the access we have as New Testament believers.

"But we all, with unveiled face, beholding as in a mirror the glory of the Lord, are being transformed into the same image from glory to glory, just as by the Spirit of the Lord." (2 Corinthians 3:18)

Again, the emphasis of Paul is for Christ's church to look like Christ Himself. If we are honest, as humans we are naturally wired to to yield in certain areas whereas other areas might be more difficult. For example, some of us are naturally more easygoing and patient. As a result, those traits come easy. Yet we might struggle more with self-discipline, for example. Whereas some may have no problem with something like unforgiveness, but might struggle with self-pity. Needless to say, no matter what our natural tendencies are, God has called us to be full and mature in Christ, leaving no area unchecked. When He has our gaze, these things happen with ease compared to trying varied methods of behavior modification.

We've all seen it, you become like those you spend time with. Have you ever become close with a new group of friends and suddenly, you begin talking like them? You might even start laughing like them and walking like them. This can be dangerous if you are running with the wrong crowd. Yet when you're spending time with Christ and with people who imitate Christ, you'll begin to imitate a godly example, thereby producing godly fruit.

"For I am the Lord, I do not change." (Malachi 3:6)

"Jesus Christ is the same yesterday, today, and forever." (Hebrews 13:8)

Let's face it, it's hard to hit a moving target. If God were always changing, it would be nearly impossible to become like Him. The second you began to emulate Him, He would change His ways and you would no longer be like Him. The fact that He remains consistently steady allows us to aim at His example and to *attain* His example. Knowing that God remains the same is a stabilizing and securing element on our end relationally. We know He is not going to respond to something a certain way today and then totally change His being and respond differently tomorrow. We are able to rest in His consistency.

I've come to see that the people that reflect His character and likeness in a full way, stay the same over the years. In other words, they are not on a rollercoaster with fluctuating character and an oscillating personality. This doesn't mean that anyone stops growing. What it *does* mean is that there is a steadiness that keeps a character-filled believer from living from valley to mountain peak and back down to the valley again.

We even see James describe God with unique language in his epistle, "Every good gift and every perfect gift is from above, and comes down from the Father of lights, with whom there is no variation or shadow of turning" (James 1:17). There is no variation with God. When you see people walk with Jesus for a long period of time, you see them experience punches from life. When that happens, you get a feel for whether or not there is "variation" in them. Those who genuinely walk in God's character have a stability that causes them to respond with grace both in good times, and bad.

A HEAVENLY ALIGNMENT

Jesus said, "Therefore you shall be perfect, just as your Father in heaven is perfect" (Matthew 5:48). Yet we also see the scriptures say, "If we say that we have no sin, we deceive ourselves, and the truth is not in us" (1 John 1:8). So what do we make of this? We must live with a balanced mindset that is subject to the full and complete lens of scripture. Yet we also must realize the standard that Jesus has called us to live out. The word *perfect* that Jesus used is actually the Greek word for *mature*. God is wanting to elevate our character to a place of maturity and fullness.

I was recently talking to a friend of mine who said he had spent time with a ministry of true acclaim and notoriety. This minister had experienced incredible prophetic visitations and was used mightily in the anointing. Yet my friend and this minister hopped in a taxi together and when the driver wasn't getting them where they needed to be, character seemed to go out the window in terms of responses and behavior. Rudeness and impatience was unashamedly displayed toward the driver by this particular minister. Point being, visitations and being used of God will not insulate you from the need to walk in godly character. A lifetime of mighty ministry can be thrown out with a short burst of character compromise. The world won't necessarily be impressed with our ministries, but they will be impressed with our integrity!

Coming into alignment with God's will for our maturity can happen rapidly when we *yield*. Of course, we can go around the wilderness for 40 years when it ought to be an 11 day journey, but God's desire is *acceleration*. Acceleration is not necessarily taking shortcuts, but rather leveraging our position in Christ will cause *character acceleration* and a rapid development into the image of Jesus.

3
CHOICES AND FEELINGS

AS WE BUILD the topic of this book, I want to make it clear: character has nothing to do with *feelings*. It can *incorporate* feelings but it's never *driven* by them. When you mirror God, it may cause good feelings in you—but it's not the determining factor of them. In the forthcoming chapters we will take a deep look at dozens of aspects of character. As we do, it's quite easy to only walk in them when we *feel like it*. Yet God gave us no feeling-based contingency in the word. Right is right, whether feelings agree or not.

> "But above all these things put on love, which is the bond of perfection. And let the peace of God rule in your hearts, to which also you were called in one body; and be thankful." (Colossians 3:14-15)

Notice, he says that *we* must put on love. That's a choice. It doesn't say that love will overtake us but that we choose to pick it up and put it on. In this case, God won't do for you what you must do for you. It's sort of like how at a certain age, you require your children to tie their own shoes. Otherwise, you would be hindering them by doing everything for them. Now, you might guide them, remind them of the how-to's and what the bunny ears should look like. But they are still doing the tying. Likewise, God requires us to put things on and put things off in the spirit. We aren't far from His help, guidance, and encouragement. Yet effort is required on our part.

All of this is available and forever opened to the people of God through Christ's death and resurrection. It is a treasury room that has been broken open. Yet you have to activate your hands and feet, walk in and grab it. You'll find as you grow and mature in the things of God it is no longer like pulling teeth to put on love. Instead, it's a joy. It's not that you *have* to walk in love and kindness but that you *get* to.

The longer you submit to your feelings as the driving force of your life, the harder it is to get out of it. Those who have been steeped in feeling and emotion-based decision making for decades, might struggle to break these cycles. This is why the Bible talks about refusing to let the sun go down on your wrath. I tell my kids, "Get off of the wave." What that means is when life happens, hurts take place, expectations are failed, and these feelings carry you—they start to build up like a wave and if you don't get off early, you get trapped in it and end up crashing with it.

Sometimes women get a bad rap, accused of making decisions by emotions and feelings, but no doubt men can be absolute emotional rollercoasters as well. It's not gender specific. It's for all to grasp. Often we let cultural norms steal from our fruit. Because of circumstances, events that take place, or the way we are treated—we let our demeanor be taken over by fruit that didn't come from God. The more you cling to the Holy Spirit, the easier it becomes to recognize that those characteristics don't belong. You become quick to cut off rotten fruit from growing in you.

You see, we were not given the right to operate in any other fruit. Our characteristics are to come from the fruit of the Spirit we see in Galatians 5. If it doesn't come from the fruit of the Spirit, then weeds will grow, Ishmaels will be produced and ugly stuff will sprout in the garden of our lives.

Feelings are a great benefit of life. I love the feeling of catching a fish or having a great coffee. But these things are merely a benefactor of the choices we make in life. They are God-given *contributors* to the makeup of humanity, but they were never intended to be the driving force of our lives. Many live by *feelings*...when *faith* is to be our mainstay. As we examine the high standard God has called us to in the coming chapters, keep in mind that the agreement of your feelings is not required. Simply yielding to the Holy Spirit and the example of Christ will cause seemingly unattainable character to be the very character you display.

PART 2
THE CONCRETE OF CHARACTER

4

DID YOU LEARN TO LOVE?

"God is love." (1 John 4:8)

GOD HIMSELF IS the purest form of love that exists. He is the substance of love. No true love is found outside of Him. Decluttering this truth is so important because of the confusion that exists in society about what true love is. In our world, imitations, look-alikes, and false versions of love exist, but the authentic substance of love can never be given, shown or experienced without God at the center-point of the equation.

You can define love with a few words, yet the definition cannot be fully given without God providing it. If you ever hear a definition of love that does not have God as the base foundation, or the exclusive lens that it's being seen through —it is false and will not produce what authentic love would produce.

I almost see love as a massive river with many small

tributaries shooting off of it. So many of the spiritual symptoms we experience are just small tributaries that have their source in love or a lack thereof. If we are not careful, we can allow spiritual logs and dams to jam the flow of the river. The scary thing is that we can continue to prophecy and minister despite our total lack of love. How? Because God's giftings and callings are without repentance. If a sinner in need of spiritual and physical healing is in front of you and you share the gospel and pray in faith for them to be healed, God most certainly will move through you. He loves the sinner. He loves the one in front of you and will move through you, *in spite of you*. Yet I pray that God would bust open our jams and allow love to flow freely in partnership with our ministries.

Real love, compared to imitation love, is like real gold compared to fool's gold. Fool's gold has no worth. It might make one excited for a moment and stir up feelings and positive emotions. Yet at the end of the day, it will be seen for what it is. Imitations won't ever produce the long-standing results that true love will. Love given without God in the picture will often backfire and produce damage.

True love cannot contradict God, for He is the subject of the matter. When you see a form of love that contradicts the Word of God, it is skewed and will backfire. It might have attributes of true love in it but the mixture of imitation-love will cause pain. Don't allow your love to be polluted but let it reflect the Lord.

"He who does not love does not know God, for God is love." (1 John 4:8)

You can only love more fully to the level you know Him more fully. Your revelation of God has a direct impact on your love levels. God does not mix love with carnality or anything else. Because He is pure, He expresses total purity in every element of His character—love included.

True love often offends those who don't understand it. Many things Jesus did were offensive to the crowd. Yet all things Jesus did were inspired by the purest love mankind had ever seen. Love doesn't seek to please the crowd primarily but to express God's exact nature. To intimately know God is to know and reflect love.

If your love meter is low, it's a good indicator that your God meter is low. You are able to gauge where you are in your spirituality based on your love exports, or lack of love exports. Love is not a single act but a lifestyle of *ways*. It's an ongoing journey and pursuit. Jesus said, "Follow me," not "Watch me for a minute." The deeper you fall into Christ the greater your love walk will become.

Bob Jones was a remarkable prophet of God, whom many of you are familiar with. He had insight from God about the abortion pill many, many years before it ever became a thing. When God showed him this, God told him to begin prophesying about it. When this took place, the devil came to him and said, "If you start to speak about this, I'll kill you." So Bob went to the Lord and the Lord said, "If you *don't* prophecy about this, *I'll* kill you." Needless to say, his fear of the devil was replaced by a healthy fear of God and he began prophesying about this pill.

After an oppressive demonic attack he died and was taken to heaven. There, he saw these two lines of people going into heaven. The line of people who were headed to heaven was small but the line going away from heaven was massive. Matthew 7 speaks of this. As he was in line for heaven, God would ask each person one question, "Did you learn to love?" It was the key question on God's heart.

So Bob approached Jesus and Jesus asked that question, "Did you learn to love?" He didn't mention Bob's ministry, his prophetic words or even the demonic attack that killed him. Instead, Jesus only cared about the love issue. When Bob came back from the visitation, it became the maxim he lived by and continually asked around the world, "Did you learn to love?" Not only that, but Bob actually passed away on Valentines Day, a day of love, in 2014. It was a clear sign from heaven that all was fulfilled and he had learned to love.

May we be a people who learn how to love God and thereby learn to love people. We ought to ooze love. "Jesus said to him, 'You shall love the Lord your God with all your heart, with all your soul, and with all your mind.' This is the first and great commandment" (Matthew 22:37-38). He doesn't stop there. He goes on to say, "And the second is like it: 'You shall love your neighbor as yourself'" (Matthew 22:39). One love leads to the next love.

"And now abide faith, hope, love, these three; but the greatest of these is love." (1 Corinthians 13:13)

"But the fruit of the Spirit is love..." (Galatians 5:22)

The premium that God places on love is evident. It is no mystery. May you encounter Jesus in such a way that love itself rubs off on you. Be branded by love. Be marked by love. Become the love that He is. The fruit of the Spirit is love, first and foremost. Obviously the list broadens from there but the first fruit listed is love indeed. It's not the fruit of you. It's not the fruit of romance, nor the fruit of society and Hollywood. It's the fruit of the Spirit—God Himself, and as you lean into Him, His love leans *into* you and *through* you.

5
LOVE, THE BIBLE WAY

> "Though I speak with the tongues of men and of angels, but have not love, I have become sounding brass or a clanging cymbal." (1 Corinthians 13:1)

THIS FAMOUS CHAPTER on love starts in a peculiar manner. Paul is talking about supernatural communication here, the ability to communicate in multiple languages and even with unknown tongues of angels. You would think nothing could steal from such a gift! Yet the sole thing that undermines a gift like this is a lack of love. He goes on to compound this truth with the next verse:

> "And though I have the gift of prophecy, and understand all mysteries and all knowledge, and though I have all faith, so that I could move mountains, but have not love, I am nothing." (1 Corinthians 13:2)

Keep in mind, Paul was talking to the Corinthians who moved heavily in the gifts of the Spirit. He actually mentioned in the first chapter of this letter, "You come short in no gift" (see 1 Corinthians 1:7). Yet he almost curbs the zeal for gifts by placing a premium on love. Why? Because love is the current from which ministry flows. Paul doesn't leave any manifestation out here. He talks about tongues, communication, faith, power, miracles, prophetic movement and more. He draws all things back to the main thing —*love*.

We run a serious risk when we depart from love yet remain in places of ministry and influence. In fact, something I've talked about repeatedly is the warning Jesus gave in Matthew 7 when He said, "Many will say to Me in that day, 'Lord, Lord, have we not prophesied in Your name, cast out demons in Your name, and done many wonders in Your name?' And then I will declare to them, 'I never knew you; depart from Me, you who practice lawlessness!'" (Matthew 7:22-23).

God's gifts are irrevocable (see Romans 11:28) as mentioned earlier. He is not taking them back. So when He gifts you, that gift will remain—often, in spite of your character or lack thereof. This is why in times past we've seen men of God with broken personal lives still operate in incredible power from the pulpit. When love is the focal point of our lives and ministries, we mitigate these risks. Paul goes on to say:

> "And though I bestow all my goods to feed the poor, and

though I give my body to be burned, but have not love, it profits me nothing." (1 Corinthians 13:3)

It might be hard to grasp this, but Paul goes so far as to say that even martyrdom is not the highest act of good…if it's not love-bathed. There are people of false religions who die for their faith, yet it is not inspired by love in any way. Love is the qualifier of all good works and the validity of any true ministry. Without it, we are merely a shell and we lack true content.

After these opening few verses in which Paul illuminates the value of love, he goes on to write eight things that love is and eight things that love is not. You have to realize that God orders the scriptures in an intentional way. Paul didn't merely create a chart with a list of eight descriptions of love and eight descriptions of the opposite of love. Instead, he wrote two things that describe what love is. Then he interjects and throws in eight descriptions of what love *is not*. And then closes out the list by throwing in the remaining six descriptions of what love *is*.

> "Love is patient, love is kind. It does not envy, it does not boast, it is not proud. It does not dishonor others, it is not self-seeking, it is not easily angered, it keeps no record of wrongs. Love does not delight in evil but rejoices with the truth. It always protects, always trusts, always hopes, always perseveres." (1 Corinthians 13:4-7 NIV)

You and I both know that if you are going to preach a

sermon, for example, and you have eight points to make *for* something and eight points to make *against* something, you typically will compartmentalize those lists. Once you finish your eight "for" points you would then rattle off your eight "against" points. However, Paul did not do this. His approach was more unorthodox. Why?

I mentioned in the last chapter how love is like a primary river and from that river flow lots of other small tributaries. This is essentially what we're seeing as Paul interjects this love list. You see that the description of what love *is not* interrupts the flow of the description of what love is. Likewise when we begin to embody what love *is not* it totally interrupts our ability to manifest and demonstrate what *love is*. It's almost as if the interruption in the order of scripture is a prophetic look at love's ability to be interrupted in our lives.

Beyond that, (not to over-spiritualize this) the biblical number eight speaks of *new order, new beginnings, and new creation*. Yet the number two can represent division and six represents the number of man. The scriptures are so multi-dimensional, I truly believe when love is interrupted, there is division that takes place among man. It could be division with that person and God *or* division with that person and another person. To bring this home and make it clear, I want to list, in the order of Paul, the descriptors that he famously lays out in this chapter.

LOVE IS

- Patient

- Kind

LOVE IS NOT

- Envious
- Arrogant
- Proud
- Rude
- Selfish
- Irritable
- Keeps no record of wrong
- Does not delight in evil

LOVE IS

- Celebratory of truth
- Able to bear all things
- Believing
- Hopeful
- Enduring
- Persevering

In keeping with the flow of Paul, I'll expound briefly in the coming chapters on each item listed prior, in the order they were originally penned in scripture. Let the summary of each love element be an invitation to put it on for yourself.

6

LOVE IS PATIENT

THE HOLY SPIRIT expressly had Paul list patience as the first attribute of love. Love is patient. Inversely, *impatience* is a lack of love. Impatience has so commonly crept into our culture from top to bottom. If anyone knows me, they know that I don't like to waste time. I like to be efficient and on top of things. Yet at times that can manifest itself as *impatience*. Yet God's character is patient and long-suffering. The Greek word for the word patience is *makrothymei* which actually means *divinely regulated patience*. In other words, it is a supernatural characteristic of God. It doesn't just happen because you prayed a two-second flare prayer. There is a self-control, continual yielding, and initiative on our part that's required.

The Greek definition of patience continues: *patience is the capacity to accept and tolerate delay*. This biblical definition is an advocate for patience in big things like jobs and relationships, as well as smaller things like traffic and bad service at a restaurant. The Greek also says that patience is *suffering without getting angry or upset, having staying power, and being the opposite of short tempered.* James chimed in on the subject with, "Let every man be swift to hear, slow to speak, slow to wrath" (James 1:19).

Notice he says, "Let everyone" be quick to listen and slow to speak, slow to anger. There are no exceptions. He didn't say, *it's only for a select few or a certain calling.* I do want to add this caveat, while embracing patience, one cannot accept laziness and live in a place of self-inflicted delay. For it is godly to be punctual, on time, prompt, and so forth. Procrastination is not of God either. While highlighting patience, I don't want to allow justification for folks in the ditch.

Character is everyday life. Patience manifests in the mundane moments of life. For example, I've got to let God's patience show up in me when I'm in line at the grocery store and the person in front of me pulls out a checkbook to pay for their items. They shuffle through their purse, flip through the checkbook, write the full name of the store, pen the date, endorse the check, then tear it out. Meanwhile I'm thinking, *I could have been through this line already. This is the 21st century. Why don't they use a card?* Yet these small moments *still require* loving patience in me.

If I'm on a flight and we are stuck on the tarmac due to weather or there is a delay, I used to get bent out of shape, but I've learned to use that time to check out and enter the secret place. As I do, accessing the fruit of the Spirit becomes natural and suddenly I'm not dominated by my circumstances but I'm *living above* my circumstances.

We can all relate to folks driving 5 mph under the speed

limit, spouses taking too long to get ready, or other little annoyances. They are things we can laugh at in hindsight, yet allowing impatience to compromise our personalities will create a domino effect of short temperedness, high blood pressure, and stress. Learn to yield to let true love's patience regulate your heart.

7

LOVE IS KIND

SOME FOLKS MIGHT BE good at patience but they struggle with kindness or basic tact. The Greek definition of kindness is *to be friendly and considerate by nature*...not just when it works for you. Love is kind, not merely when you have an audience. It's kind always, for God is the same yesterday, today and forever. It's easy to be kind when you've been treated well and everything is smooth. It's another thing to be kind when you've been mistreated.

To be kind means to be generous, pleasant, gentle, enjoyable, and likable. I'm not pointing fingers, but we've all seen preachers who are harsh and unpleasant. Obviously, there is a time and a place to be straightforward and to spill hard hitting truth. Yet kindness remains an attribute we ought to walk in. Kindness is satisfying to be around. However, it doesn't mean that we are to be people-pleasers with no backbone.

Jesus was sharing with some folks and began to describe

the last days. Interestingly, He said, "And because lawlessness will abound, *the love of many will grow cold*" (Matthew 24:12 emphasis added). This has become the norm of society. In an earth that's been frozen over with cold, rude, hard hearted behavior...kindness is like a warm campfire—signaling safety and comfort to those who will come near. Let this attribute be your testimony!

8

LOVE IS NOT ENVIOUS

LOVE IS NOT JEALOUS. Jealousy is the pursuit of a person or thing with one's heart *completely* set on it. This is an opposing current that cuts off the flow of authentic love, thereby making us warped in our display *of* God and our connection *to* God. Now, you might wonder, *but the Bible says God is a jealous God.* Or Paul said, *covet and be jealous for the spiritual gifts.* It's a good question, because the word for jealous is the same word in the Greek in all those instances. Yet their meanings vary greatly. The truth is, the only upright jealousy is jealousy that has had the heart and mind of God applied to it.

The only safe jealousy is when it's yielded to the heart of God. Generally, this holy jealousy is vertical. It's the heart of God flowing in you and through you. The only way to take your envy-temperature, so to speak, is to ask yourself *what is fueling my jealousy?* If jealousy is connected to and toward the things of God, then it's safe and can be healthy. When jealousy is geared horizontally, you begin to operate outside of authentic love.

If you feel an unhealthy jealousy rise up in your heart, *immediately* ask God to deal with it and remove it from you. Don't delay. Even in ministry and at high levels of Christendom, jealousy can be pervasive. Yet love expels it. Don't let jealousy be your demise. Success is not determined by the standards of people. The smile of the Father is our place of contentment. Our food is to do His will.

I was at a conference once and a multi-millionaire and his friends were in a greenroom with me. This man had a heart to fund kingdom works and would give massive amounts of wealth to gospel-centered causes. He would do it under the radar—not for the praise of men. In this green room, this man asked me to pray for him. When I prayed for him, I saw a red carpet being rolled out for him. I told him that his status in heaven was known in heaven much like Cornelius who had a memorial in heaven because of his generosity.

Interestingly enough, I didn't have much at all to give him about his future. It just wasn't there. The word was very much just about his position in heaven. A year later the man died, unexpectedly. I say all that to say this, God was highlighting this man's heavenly status and position. Why? Because it was what mattered most. Life is not about comparisons, competitions, and climbing on shoulders to get to the top. Those things are fueled by jealousy, when at the end of the day it has always been about love.

9

LOVE IS NOT ARROGANT

THE GREEK WORD for arrogant or boastful is *perpereuetai*. What does it mean? It means *to brag, to be vainglorious, excessively proud of oneself or one's achievements, and to need excessive attention*. Now, the root of this is often insecurity—which is another issue. Yet I think most of us would agree that there are very few things as distasteful as someone who is completely full of themselves. When you do what you do as a grab for attention, you've stepped outside of love.

Love and humility have a zero tolerance policy toward arrogance. Boastfulness does not well represent the character of God. Arrogance is one of those character flaws that both the church and people outside of the church can all agree is nasty. As a result, the opposite of arrogance (love) is celebrated by the church and by the world and actually serves to build the reputation of Jesus in a positive manner. Arrogance will isolate you. It shifts trust from God to you, which is dangerous.

The reason love and arrogance are polar opposites is simply because love pulls your eyes off of you and onto those near you. Yet arrogance puts your eyes on you and attempts to pull everyone else's eyes on you also. A cocky attitude is felt in a room like unbearable humidity; everyone feels it and everyone knows it. Yet a loving persona is like a beautiful fragrance, everyone knows that it's there and they're blessed by it.

10

LOVE IS NOT PROUD

THE GREEK ORIGIN for *proud* is the word *physioutai*. This means egotistical, swelled up, having or revealing an exaggerated sense of one's importance or abilities. Pride runs in tandem with arrogance. A proud person has a way of bringing the conversation to themselves and if the chat shifts to other things, they will attempt to bring it back to them. The qualities of love are mostly exports of God's character but pride brings it all back to self. Pride is the founder of the earthly trinity, as they say: *me, myself, and I.*

To pride, the goal of life is to import attention and applause. Pride relies upon itself. Self-trust is a scary place to be. Pride elevates a person, which actually results in demotion. This is what happened with Satan. In fact, the scripture says, "Pride goes before destruction, and a haughty spirit before a fall" (Proverbs 16:18).

James also hit this subject and penned, "God resists the proud, but gives grace to the humble" (James 4:6). Favor, destiny and fulfillment in God can be retracted very quickly when pride enters. I know a minister in another nation who is incredibly gifted and powerful in the Lord. By the Spirit, He would command a thing and suddenly demons would manifest and mass exorcisms would take place. Thousands would gather to hear his preaching. Yet over time, pride crept in. As a result, the machine is still running but not at the efficiency and effectiveness that it once was. Pride will tear down what God has built up. Disgrace follows pride. God opposes and fights against those who are immersed in pride.

Now, you might say, "I'm at rock bottom. I have nothing and am nothing. Pride isn't my issue at all." While that may be true, know that as God brings elevation and an *uplifting* into your life, you'll have the honor of shaking off pride and remaining in love. In fact, many people have little, yet still are in pride over the little they have. No one is exempt from putting off pride and remaining in love. It is a thing to be fought against in the big things and in the small day to day decisions.

11

LOVE IS NOT RUDE

ASCHÉMONEÓ IS the Greek word for rude that means *to act unbecomingly, improperly, or to be dishonoring*. The Greek describes that when we are acting rude we are out of the proper *shape and form*. Love is to be our shape and form, yet rudeness causes us to be out of whack. Imagine using a coffee cup with a rounded bottom and a lip that you couldn't drink out of. It would be useless. You can't set it down, you can't drink from it—it's purpose is defeated by its lack of form. Likewise, rudeness causes our character to be malformed.

Whether the situation is favorable or not, we are to be tactful and honorable. Keep honor high in your life. Don't allow familiarity to breed contempt. Kindness is your antidote to rudeness. When writing a text message, for example, it's very easy to come across as rude when you didn't intend to at all. The Bible instructs us to avoid the very appearance of evil (see 1 Thess. 5:22). When writing on social media, texting, legal paperwork, or email—it's very easy to forget about tone. This could be a deal breaker, door closer, or door opener. Don't let rudeness enter your tone. Telling the truth is not the entirety of the biblical command. Telling the truth *in love* is the fullness of the instruction. We see Jesus giving rebuke in Revelation, but it was done in love. He would point out good things and commendable things as well. He wasn't rude, nor should we be. It isn't an attractive quality—it's not a quality at all. Let love purge you of tactless behavior and infill you with loving honor.

12

LOVE IS NOT SELFISH

LOVE DOES NOT DEMAND its own way. We've all been here. Selfishness might just be the most relatable plague to all humanity. We were born in this place. May we be people to take a back seat and not insist on our own way. Jesus said, "Greater love has no one than this, than to lay down one's life for his friends" (John 15:13). Selfishness will produce death. Let's call it what it is. It's outside of the character of God. When we plant selfish seeds we experience a rotten harvest of headache, heartache and confusion. Yet the inverse is true, planting seeds of love will produce a harvest of love.

At first, refusing to walk in selfishness can be difficult. It seems costly. Yet when you press ahead, deny self, and cling to the cross—you start to see the fruit and the reward of this life. When you taste it, you'll be motivated to continue in it. The reward of selflessness is far greater than the consequences of selfishness.

"Let nothing be done through selfish ambition or conceit, but in lowliness of mind let each esteem others better than himself. Let each of you look out not only for his own interests, but also for the interests of others." (Philipians 2:3-4)

Notice, he did say that we are to look out for our own interests also. A call to be selfless is not a call to neglect yourself or become self-deprecating. To give you an example, John G. Lake is a general in the faith whom I admire greatly. In fact, my daughter's middle name is Lake, after him. He had an incredible revelation of God and His power. In South Africa, the crowds pressed in around him so much that instead of laying hands on everyone, Lake spotted a tree stump, laid hands on it and prayed, and told everyone that if they would go touch that tree stump they would be healed. It was much like Paul laying hands on handkerchiefs and those who touched the handkerchief were healed and delivered. Sure enough, folks began getting healed by the masses at this tree stump.

John and his family moved to Spokane, Washington and began establishing healing rooms. It became the healthiest city in the United States and Lake was actually given a practicing medical license by local authorities because of the results his ministry was seeing. However, his first wife, Jenny Lake, actually died of malnutrition and neglect prematurely. Reason being, she was so giving of herself and invested in the ministry, that she failed to care for her own self.

There is a balance to be had. Physical fitness, good sleep,

and good nutrition are all elements of this whole picture. Taking care of business in this way is not an act of selfishness. In fact, by taking care of your own temple and soul, you are positioned to selflessly lay down your life for those in your care.

Yet in our western culture, and frankly in all cultures, sliding into selfishness and self-seeking is a massive issue. Authentic love in the midst of a culture that is self-obsessed stands out as a mighty testimony to the love of Christ in us. Jesus Himself said, "By this all will know that you are My disciples, if you have love for one another" (John 13:35).

13

LOVE IS NOT IRRITABLE

TO BE irritable means *to have a sharp edge, to be easily angered, or to be quick to lose temper.* This is big! We might read this list and do everything really well. We might say, "Yeah, I prefer others. I am not full of myself." But at the same time, we might lose it quickly in traffic or explode if something is out of the order we prefer. To be easily provoked is to be unloving. You can spend 12-hours selflessly feeding the poor, yet in your car on the way home you blow up when someone cuts you off.

"So then, my beloved brethren, let every man be swift to hear, slow to speak, slow to wrath" (James 1:19). It takes a long, long time for love to become angered or irritated. Proverbs says, "He who is slow to anger is better than the mighty" (Proverbs 16:32). You might feel irritable at times. A lack of sleep or not having food in your system can make one *hangry*, as they say. But we've got to get better at mastering these feelings and being slow to irritation.

We've all dropped the ball on this subject a number of times. For me, there are times where I need the Holy Ghost and about 8 angels to keep me from being irritated. Little things like *ticking noises* or *loud chewing* are like fingernails on a chalkboard to me. I love stillness. The busy, fidgety and twitchy types can get on my nerves if I'm not careful. I was once on a flight going to Columbia and myself and a buddy of mine upgraded to first class. Because it was a longer flight than normal, I was looking forward to peace, rest, and spending time in the secret place.

A Columbian man and his wife came aboard first class and sat right next to me. They might not have been Columbian drug lords, but they certainly looked the part. They were clearly wealthy and blinged out from head to toe. When they sat down they were super hostile with one another, he was angry and ripping into his wife. It was so loud that security came on board and warned him that they would remove him if he didn't cool down. He just sort of tilted his head to the side and pretended to go to sleep, ignoring them completely. I was thinking, *don't fall for it. This guy is faking being calm. As soon as we take off he is going to explode again.*

Sure enough, as soon as the wheels lifted off the tarmac, the guy came alive again. He started yelling at his wife, stomping his feet to the point that you could feel it on the floor of the plane. If someone is loud, I can use noise cancelling headphones, but the stomping and the scene that was being made couldn't be ignored. Everyone in first class was aware of the guy. At one point during dinner he even held his butter knife to his wife's neck. I looked around and saw a small female stewardess and a petite male flight attendant. I knew if something got out of hand they wouldn't be able to handle this guy. I was getting irritated to the highest degree.

The flight attendant took the man's drink order. He didn't speak English but he knew how to say, "Vodka on the rocks." The flight attendant warned the man that security wouldn't allow him to have alcohol on the flight. He was visibly upset by their refusal to give him alcohol. The male flight attendant came over to me, took my order, and I thanked him for not giving the man alcohol. He could see that I was bigger and able to handle myself and said, "If this guy gets out of hand, would you be willing to stand in and help?" Of course I was willing! In my mind, that was a green light. If things needed to be done, I could detain him without a lawsuit from the airline.

Five minutes later he is stomping and throwing a tantrum. I reached across the aisle, popped him in the shoulder with the flat part of my hand. He looked at me. It was enough to get his attention. I looked through him. I wasn't happy and he knew it. I communicated to him that he had better cut it out. I think everyone in first class breathed a sigh of relief. It wasn't a few minutes later and he went right back to stomping and yelling. I popped him on the shoulder again and basically said, "What part of this don't you understand?" Without getting into it, I wasn't nearly as nice about it this time whatsoever. He got the message this time and was fine for the rest of the flight. He certainly didn't like me, and

I could have handled the situation much better. My motivation was irritation when love would have been an upgrade.

No matter what the scenario is, we all could benefit from clinging to love and shedding irritation. Whether it's a reckless man on a flight or a family member who didn't load the dishwasher correctly. When we are easily irritated, the people around us feel that they are walking on eggshells. Yet when we are slow to anger, we are a joy to be around. We are trusted by man and affirmed by God.

14

LOVE KEEPS NO RECORD OF WRONG

I'VE SEEN this area lacking in a number of ways. Love does not keep a "black book," as it were. To keep a record of wrongs means *to keep account, charge with, save, download, and store up offenses.* Unless you live in a bubble by yourself, wrong will be done to you. You cannot escape it. Yet love forgets it and moves on.

When a person is done wrong, their first temptation is often to justify their bitterness by pretending that the offense was uniquely disgusting. Yet all experience deep offense and the standard of forgiveness does not change. Christ offered forgiveness to those who killed Him while He was still nailed to the cross...and they hadn't even asked for forgiveness! You look so much like Jesus when you refuse to take notes when people sin against you. The old saying is true, "Don't allow sin *against you* to produce sin *in you.*"

If you keep a record of wrong, the full potential of people in your life can't be realized. Many years ago I was done wrong in ministry. I won't get into it, but things were not pretty. I wanted to just cut this person off. That's my nature. I don't like weeds and I'm okay with leaving things behind. I asked my friend, Shawn Williamson, what I should do about it. He was a neutral third party and a good source for advice. He said, "I'll tell you this. This life is a long haul. You will likely need each other in some form or fashion down the road. Love them. Forget the wrong." It was awesome advice.

Since then, we've had people come against us. Many times I simply didn't bring it up or mention it to them. Over time we've seen people come full circle and end up becoming big supporters. Yet if I had cut them off or kept a record of wrong that would have never happened. It won't just benefit the people in your midst but *you yourself* if you are willing to let offense flow off of you like water on a duck's back.

Rolland Buck was a wonderful minister of the Lord from a generation prior. He was a pastor and one day he was studying in his office and had an encounter with God that opened up his life to visitations with angels that spanned throughout his life. It is well documented. He talked about how he had a conversation with an angel once and the angel said to him, "The records in heaven keep no account of the wrongs of believers."

Now, don't get me wrong. We still need repentance and so forth, but God is not keeping track of the failures of men. Rolland said he inquired and the angel said that even the account of the failures of men in the Bible have been penned for our sake, yet they aren't recorded in heaven. Even in

Hebrews we see the "hall of faith" (see Hebrews 11). In it, the Holy Spirit inspired the author to write about the various legends of the Bible, be it David, Abraham, Noah and more. Yet through this New Covenant lens, the writer does not bring out their shortcomings and failure—even though they had plenty. He emphasizes their great faith. God keeps no list by which He judges men. He judges us by Christ's blood.

Let me put it like this, picture the desktop of your computer. When you delete an old file, it goes to your trash bin. At that point you still have to empty that trash bin. In the Kingdom, it's as though the moment a file is deleted, there is no trash bin holding the record. It's gone. "For I will be merciful to their unrighteousness, and their sins and their lawless deeds I will remember no more" (Hebrews 8:12).

From the Old Testament to the New, you see God's heart to forgive *completely*. You also see our call to be like Him. To be Christlike is to forgive and forget. This also applies to your own self. In the same way that you don't have the right to refuse to forgive someone else, you don't have the right to refuse to forgive yourself. Some don't have an issue with forgiving other people, yet they are hard on themselves. Forgive people, forgive yourself, and walk in love completely.

15

LOVE DOES NOT DELIGHT IN EVIL

LOVE DOES NOT FIND entertainment nor excitement in sin and evil. Whether it is the lust of the flesh, the lust of the eyes, or the pride of life—the world tends to find excitement in these things. Yet love does not find delight in them. Many think that our antidote to sin is white knuckling our way through life. Yet this is not so. Love is the solution. Love has the ability to restrain us in ways that rules and regulations do not.

If you find out about bad news, someone being hurt, or a messy situation unfolding—love causes you to have *sympathy*. Perhaps you have seen a callous person laugh at calamity and tragedy when they find out about it. This is the opposite of God's nature. The Lord would have us to be tender and sensitive to the plight of others.

God's standards don't change. Society and culture *never* dictate what righteousness is. Obviously, we don't want to be dogmatic and rude in any way, but the Bible is clear about what righteousness is and what it is not. We don't get to make that up as we go along. In fact, if we are walking in love —we won't want to!

A love for God and His Word will cause us to see people through His eyes. We will recognize what is best for them and it's easy to see that sin and counter-scriptural lifestyles won't do it for them. As we walk in love and carry out this lifestyle, we won't find ourselves rejoicing in bad things but we will rejoice in better things, which we will begin to unpack in the forthcoming chapter.

16

LOVE REJOICES IN TRUTH

PAUL WRAPS up his interjection on what love is *not* and continues with what love is. "Love does not delight in evil but rejoices with the truth. It always protects, always trusts, always hopes, always perseveres" (1 Corinthians 13:7). Love rejoices with truth for truth is Him. Jesus is the way, the truth and the life (see John 14:16). Truth in this passage on love means *the quality or state of being accurate and verifiable*. It further means *not merely spoken truth* but the *reality* and *substance* of truth itself.

When there is injustice, evil, lies and deception—love doesn't find joy. Love enjoys and celebrates truth, despite the setting, circumstances and crowd. Love throws a party when truth is revealed. Love and truth work together in perfect harmony. They say that without truth, love is too soft and without love, truth is too harsh. The apostle known for *love* is John. He boldly declared, as an embodiment of these things, "I have no greater joy than to hear that my children walk in truth" (3 John 1:4). Imagine that, the love apostle himself finds incredible happiness in truth.

My son is an exceptional basketball player. Not to be too biased or anything, but he really is fantastic on the court. If you're familiar with the sport, it's easy to see that he has a very natural, fluid shot. He's always winning free throw contests and excels in competition. One day another kid said something critical about his shot. It wasn't true. It was a remark that wasn't based on reality but was just to mess with my son. I could tell it was bothering him and I didn't like that a lie was attempting to be set in his mind.

I asked him, "How well does the kid who told you this shoot?" He replied, "He doesn't make much."

"So you mean to tell me a guy who can't shoot is being critical of your shot? When the guy can shoot as good as you, then you might listen to him. Until then, your shot is working and it's great," I said.

We ended that lie and he was free. It's a small example, but what could have happened is my son could have hung onto that lie and developed a complex. From there he might start to alter his shot in unnecessary ways and damage his game. These same principles apply to bigger lies in life also. Lies about our appearance, personality, past, future, family, and so forth, can be planted causing compromise, complexes and ultimately...*calamity*.

See, in the garden of Eden, the enemy gained access to Adam and Eve through deceit and the manipulation of truth. The only ground that he has to stand on in our lives is the ground we give him by believing his lies. The Bible even refers to him as the father of lies. Naturally, love will reject and attack anything from this origin.

The marriage of love and truth has existed eternally. When you host a habitation of truth, the enemy has no ticket in. When we walk in love, we develop an appetite for truth and will lose our tolerance for lies. We will begin to see just how much half-truths and lies cost us. Lies and deception work in tandem. They are the two tracks running parallel on the same railroad, so to speak.

When someone is deceptive, they often think they are in the clear because it's not a flat out lie. Yet 99% truth with 1% deception mixed in is still a corruption that leads to destruction. That 1% deception will corrupt the 99% health. There's a name for a half-truth...*a lie*. When we buy into these things, it's a dangerous place to be. The problem with deception is that you don't know you are in deception. You think you're on track. Yet there are a number of ways to get past deception. Some of those include:

- Spend time in the secret place
- Let God search your heart
- Examine the fruit of what you are believing
- Be willing to let go of things you've bought into heavily
- Spot and uproot seeds of deception

I truly believe there is a company of people rising up who will walk in such a spirit of truth it will be tangible.

They will have no tolerance for lies, deceit and exaggeration. We can see from John 8 that where there is no truth, there can never be true freedom. The depth at which truth is known is the extent to which freedom is experienced. Truth known, equates to freedom experienced.

17

LOVE PROTECTS

SOME TRANSLATIONS SAY, "Love bears all things." The Greek word for *bears* means *to cover as with a roof*, or *to protect as with a shield*. Love is a defense mechanism. It's refreshing when you come across people who operate in this. They don't expose and wound. They cover and protect. Love is life's greatest teammate. It mourns when you mourn and rejoices when you rejoice. Love looks at the vulnerable and instead of taking advantage or exploiting or further wounding, love protects and covers.

We see a wonderful example of this in scripture. Noah fell short, became drunk and wound up naked and exposed. His sons, in love, acted on the situation. The Bible says, "Shem and Japheth took a garment, laid it on both their shoulders, and went backward and covered the nakedness of their father. Their faces were turned away, and they did not see their father's nakedness" (Genesis 9:23).

To be clear, love does not conceal sin and compromise,

that would further steep people in their sin. But love preserves and upholds the person in the stability of God with the filter of honor—always seeing people through the lens of God's full grace, mercy and love. Love wants people to be guarded and in their full potential. Perhaps the most famous example of this would be with the *good Samaritan*. He came along, helped one who was vulnerable, and invested in a person without the guarantee of any return whatsoever. It was a selfless act of protective love that inspires us to do likewise.

18

LOVE BELIEVES ALL THINGS

THE GREEK UNDERSTANDING of this passage is that love has *firm belief* and wants to rely on the people being around it. Love is not hyper-skeptical nor finger pointing, in other words. Love is not suspicious. Love invests belief and trust into someone, which as a result supernaturally empowers them. Often, the operation of good transforms evil into good.

There are times when someone's track record might not warrant trust or credibility. Yet love is able to trust them, which often empowers them into a trustworthy way of life. God has set up the system so that in trusting someone, they actually become trustworthy. Now, there are exceptions and obviously this is not a license to be unwise or to be taken advantage of. Boundaries still exist. Yet one of these manifestations of love is the supernatural ability to put faith in people and the God who is working in them.

Simple things like trusting someone to borrow your car

calls them to a higher standard and level of responsibility. In the scriptures, when the master gave talents to his servants, they were trusted with what he gave them. It was an act of love to delegate these talents. Fleshing out this principle will better express the love of Christ and free us from lives of suspicion and skepticism.

Often we put distrust on people in our present, due to wounds in our past. As a result it hinders relationships and limits people from walking in their destiny. The manifestation of someone's destiny might, in part, depend on you being willing to trust them with assignments and resources.

All in all, the gold you gain from trusting people *far* exceeds the hurt you might experience from trusting people. If you trust no one you get nothing. Yet if you trust 10 people, one person might hurt you and fail you, but nine will blow you away with what they've done with your trust. It far outweighs shutting down, isolating, limiting love, and thereby limiting trust.

19

LOVE HOPES ALL THINGS

"Now hope does not disappoint, because the love of God has been poured out in our hearts by the Holy Spirit who was given to us." (Romans 5:5)

HOPE HERE MEANS *TO ANTICIPATE, expect or desire for a certain thing to come.* This is an empowering characteristic of God who is love. Love is in a continual state of expectation. It can certainly be self-applied. Yet I do believe this is external. It's a flow from you to others. Hope is not solely for the benefit of self, but to the world around you. Hope is one of the chain links that can strengthen us in times of trouble.

Yet the exporting of hope to others is a powerful face of love. When you put your hope in people, it authorizes them to reach higher. Now, that does not mean you put an unhealthy expectation on people to perform in order to be accepted. But it's a hope placed on others to call them to walk in the fullness of what God has for them. This is a powerful tool in seasons of delay. People can sense and feel the effects of the hope you're releasing on them. It's refreshing. We ought to be *buckets of hope* in the midst of a hopeless generation.

If you think about it, there is nothing loving about being beat down, depressed, and always railing about how bad things are and how they will never get better. Generally speaking, the people we know who are constantly negative are not among the loving bunch. Yet those who are full of love automatically tend to be positive, hopeful and filled with anticipation. Why? Because love *always* hopes.

20

LOVE ENDURES ALL THINGS AND LOVE PERSEVERES

I WANT to couple these last two attributes together as they are similar in nature. Put simply, love *remains, survives and lasts*. Even in times of failure and disappointment, love does not give up. It locks arms with you and does not quit. Look, it's really easy to endure good things, great things, and happy things. Yet it's when the storm comes that endurance comes into play.

"A friend loves at all times." (Proverbs 17:17)

Often we think that *staying power* comes from gritting our teeth and stomping our feet. Yet staying power comes through a soul surrendered to the love of God. The only fail-proof power we have is love, for *love never fails*. Through the generations, the sustaining love of God never ends. We are the continuing vessels keeping Christ's love pertinent in the earth. Love is a light that never fades and an ocean that never ends. Because of this eternal quality, we always have it to lean on in times of trial and hardship.

As long as you will stay on the road of love, it only gets more beautiful the longer you stay on it. With God, all things go from glory to glory and from strength to strength. They increase in beauty and fulfilment and every other attribute in God. Any other road you choose that's not true love will always diminish in greatness, decrease in favor, and many bad endings are possible. Yet the true love of God is an endless road of bliss.

> "For I am persuaded that neither death nor life, nor angel, nor principalities, nor powers, nor things present nor things to come, nor height nor depth, nor any other created thing, shall be able to separate us from the love of God which is in Christ Jesus our Lord." (Romans 8:38-39)

PART 3

THE PILLARS OF CHARACTER

21

THE POWER OF PURITY

"That He might sanctify and cleanse her with the washing of water by the word, that He might present her to Himself a glorious church, not having spot or wrinkle or any such thing, but that she should be holy and without blemish." (Ephesians 5:26-27)

WE KNOW that apart from the grace, blood, and resurrection of Jesus, we have no purity and holiness. Yet walking in a consecrated manner is a cooperation. The redemptive realities that Christ provided must be appropriated and applied by us. Notice what Paul told Timothy, "Do not lay hands on anyone hastily, nor share in other people's sins; keep yourself pure" (1 Timothy 5:22). The phrase, "Keep yourself pure," is a call for us to participate in purity. This doesn't mean that we keep ourselves pure in our own strength but in partnership with Christ's desire to purify us.

"Let no one despise your youth, but be an example to the believers in word, in conduct, in love, in spirit, in faith, in purity." (1 Timothy 4:12)

"Blessed are the pure in heart, for they shall see God." (Matthew 5:8)

Purity is a pathway. What is this pathway leading us to? To seeing more of God in our lives. Some might think that being a *seer* is all about having a unique gift. Granted, there are special gifts to see certain things in the spirit. Yet one lesser known facet of God is that *purity* actually opens us up to seeing God and His activity in our lives in a new way.

"Who may ascend into the hill of the Lord? Or who may stand in His holy place? He who has clean hands and a pure heart, who has not lifted up his soul to an idol, nor sworn deceitfully." (Psalm 24:3-4)

Clean hands refer to our outward deeds. A pure heart refers to inward motives. God is interested in both. The pharisees were known for being *white washed tombs* as Jesus said. They had outward deeds that appeared to be holy and religious, yet inside they were full of dead men's bones. Their motivations were off. The fuel behind their lives was pride, arrogance, appearance, and haughtiness. Yet Christ came to purify us, not merely outwardly, but in the secret, inward motivation of our hearts.

"Therefore you shall be perfect, just as your Father in heaven is perfect." (Matthew 5:48)

I'll never forget, I was just born again. Weeks old in the Spirit. I got saved with a guy who was fresh out of the rave scene. Somehow we ended up at a Bible study under a really twisted teacher. He misused this passage out of Matthew 5 and said that if you ever sin, you can miss salvation. Yet this is not what the passage is saying. Instead, it's saying that our standard and high calling is to emulate our Father God.

Jesus does not lower the bar to accommodate humanity's failures. He didn't say, "Be deficient, even though your Father in Heaven is perfect." No, He actually invites us into a God-like lifestyle of purity and holiness. Peter echoed these realities, "But as He who called you is holy, you also be holy in all your conduct, because it is written, 'Be holy, for I am holy'" (1 Peter 1:15-16).

22

A CULTURE OF HONOR

HONOR IS a total reflection of the character of God and we are to be a people of honor. By definition, honor is *to esteem, cherish, appreciate, revere, look up to and think highly of a person*. Paul said, "Be kindly affectionate to one another with brotherly love, in honor giving preference to one another" (Romans 12:10). Some translations actually say to *outdo* one another with honor. Giving honor and preference to one another makes room for God to work. The Greek breakdown of this word *honor* that's used here means to evaluate a price, to pay respect, appreciate, and look up to. This passage in Romans 12 is specifically referring to honoring those *within* the body of Christ.

Yet Peter picks up where Paul leaves off and writes about how we are to honor *all* people, in the church and outside of the church. "Honor all people. Love the brotherhood. Fear God. Honor the king" (1 Peter 2:17). Interestingly enough, the word for honor here is *different* when referring to *all* people.

It actually means to *assign* a value, to esteem and to cherish. Did you catch the difference? When honoring believers, we are simply *evaluating* their value. Christ is in them. We honor the established residence of Christ. Yet when dealing with unbelievers, we are actually *assigning* and choosing to see the value that they possess through the lens of God. It's an honor of a prophetic variety.

Honor is a spiritual protocol that allows our lives to fire on all cylinders. When honor is absent, it's like attempting to push water through a kinked hose. We see Paul continuing to press these realities to the Philippian church, "Let nothing be done through selfish ambition or conceit, but in lowliness of mind let each *esteem others* better than himself" (Philippians 2:3 emphasis added). We see in the world, and even in the church, people jockeying for position and attempting to climb shoulders to get to the top. This reduces relationships to competition, and is completely the inverse of the biblical prescription of honor.

In the Kingdom, the path to promotion is in preferring others and elevating them, while you take the low road. It's a beautiful thing. We are called to love people who sometimes act in a dishonorable way. We can only do this through the prophetic lens of God. It takes a very secure person to honor in the way we are called to honor others. Insecurity will attempt to dam the river of honor in one's life. Why? Because insecurity attempts to keep you high and others low in order to keep its comfortable place.

Yet you reap what you sow. As a result, insecurity will reap dishonor, which will cause one to sew more dishonor—

it's a deadly cycle. Insecurities' best friend is jealousy. *Jealousy, comparison, and insecurity* all run together—working to stomp out honor in our midst. These things can masquerade in many ways. Joking can become jabs, and sharing testimonies can become a stage to brag. We can candy coat it all we want, but at the end of the day insecurities will stop up the flow of honor and leave us lacking in more ways than one.

God can only elevate you in honor to the level at which you live in honor toward others. When we honor others, the Lord honors us. When God honors someone and places favor on their life, it's very evident. It's tangible and unstoppable. The benefits of honor are not the sole or primary motivations for us to export honor. We honor because God wants us to. We honor because it's the byproduct of love. Yet by aligning with honor, we attract favor, blessing and in fact, honor is linked to long life. One of the most powerful promises given in Exodus was to honor mother and father, resulting in extended life.

Sometimes people will start in honor, and over time devolve because of familiarity. Familiarity can breed contempt. When you become closely associated with a person or thing, it can cause a loss of respect. You see *behind the curtain,* so to speak, and your findings can cause you to lose your sense of honor toward that person. Yet honor is to be given despite familiarity. Our honor levels don't depend on familiarity levels or lack thereof.

Honor opens doors, blesses the recipients and blesses the giver. We must be careful, for doors that opened through honor can close because of a lack of it. Honor is a true outflow of Christ's character in you that can't be overlooked. A culture of honor is to be cultivated, built and developed in our homes, lives, families, ministries and communities. The world will be better for it.

23

THE HUMBLE HEART

"Take my yoke upon you and learn from me, for I am gentle and humble in heart." (Matthew 11:29 NIV)

HUMILITY ACCOMPANIES HONOR. It's hard to lift people above yourself without the virtue of humility. To me, there's nothing more beautiful than to see a person walking in humility. In fact, it's my personal favorite. It's the characteristic that stands out to me the most. I'll never forget, I was in prayer several years ago and I was really hung up on the passage that described Moses talking face to face with God as a friend. I had a holy jealousy toward this encounter.

I remember inquiring of the Lord, "What enabled Moses to have this unique position with you? Throughout Scripture I don't see anyone who has had this face to face access." The Spirit said, "What was the only attribute that set Moses apart from anyone else in the earth?" He answered my question with a question. I knew the answer:

"Now the man Moses was very humble, more than all men who were on the face of the earth." (Numbers 12:3)

Moses had access that others did not have because Moses had a humility that no one else had. He didn't have an ego. The beautiful thing about a humble person is you can dump praise on them all day. They will appreciate it, but it won't inflate them. It all goes back to Jesus.

Humility means that one is God-reliant instead of self-reliant. Humility is not about beating yourself up or being self-destructive. It's about refusing to be self-sufficient but instead, God-sufficient. Humility is not thinking less of yourself, but thinking of yourself less. Humility is resistless, meek, and lowly. It's submissive and quick to obey the voice of the Lord. Humility is not self-focused nor is it wrapped up in self-praise.

Humble people are pliable and form into shape quicker than those who still deal with pride. Those with humble hearts will access their destiny quicker than those who are far from lowliness. If you think of a lump of clay on the potter's wheel, the best clay is pliable clay. It's easy to mold in a quick manner. Yet pride is like clay that has to be broken, re-watered, and re-worked continually.

Personally, I watch for humility in people. If I see humility in a person, I can run with that person. If a person walks in humility above all else, they will go far. I would take humility over gifts, abilities, and skills. A humble person is adaptable, correctable, and able to be lifted up.

Yet someone in pride doesn't think they have any issues to begin with. Humility is attractive to God and man. It's attractive to sinners and saints alike. Meek people are exalted quicker and hold positions longer and more consistently. Jesus Himself said, "Blessed are the meek, for they will inherit the earth" (Matthew 5:5 NIV). Solomon understood this and declared:

"Humility is the fear of the Lord; its wages are riches and honor and life." (Proverbs 22:4)

Over and over you hear people complaining about not being far enough along or not experiencing the acceleration they would like. It's often because they are bypassing the most important step to get there: humility. James said, "Humble yourselves before the Lord, and he will lift you up" (James 4:10). Peter also said, "Humble yourselves, therefore, under God's mighty hand, that he may lift you up in due time" (1 Peter 5:6).

When God honors you and elevates you because of humility, He sustains you there. If you lift yourself up, you must sustain yourself in that place. Many people build their own machine that they themselves have to keep running. At that point, it turns and ends up running them. This sort of self-exaltation results in destruction. Yet when God lifts you up, He is the one who sustains you and keeps you. For the same power that got you there will hold you there. The humility that exalts you is the humility that keeps you there safely. We never graduate past humility. It is without question, the first and final state of being and it's everything in between.

> 24
>
> EXUDING EXCELLENCE

"Then this Daniel distinguished himself above the governors and satraps, because an excellent spirit was in him." (Daniel 6:3)

DANIEL'S HALLMARK was not his ability to pull strings, manipulate his way to the top, or be the best looking guy. No, his unique marker was his excellence. Anything God manufactures is done with excellence. It's something we need to come into alignment with more and more. It won't happen overnight. It's a process of cultivating and developing God's perspective on our various ventures. The book of Daniel goes on to say, "and the king gave thought to setting him over the whole realm" (Daniel 6:3).

These passages are cornerstones for marketplace ministry. Here's why: the world doesn't necessarily recognize the Spirit of God at work in you. Yet, they recognize a spirit of excellence. They might not understand why you pray during your lunch break, but they understand that you're putting out better numbers than anybody in the department. Excellence is undeniable. It caused promotion to an unprecedented degree in Daniel's life and can do the same for you.

> "There is a man in your kingdom in whom is the Spirit of the Holy God. And in the days of your father, light and understanding and wisdom, like the wisdom of the gods, were found in him; and King Nebuchadnezzar your father —your father the king—made him chief of the magicians, astrologers, Chaldeans, and soothsayers. Inasmuch as an excellent spirit, knowledge, understanding, interpreting dreams, solving riddles, and explaining enigmas were found in this Daniel, whom the king named Belteshazzar, now let Daniel be called, and he will give the interpretation." (Daniel 5:11-12)

Excellence was Daniel's mainstay. The word excellence here in the Hebrew means *greatest, preeminent, distinguished, outstanding, top-tier, surpassing*. In the previous chapter, we dialed in on humility and you might think, "These things don't sound like humility." Yet it's actually humility that positions us to walk in this top-tier spirit of excellence. People who chase after a distinguished position will often compromise to get there. But people who walk in humility will receive and walk in excellence in an effortless way.

Excellence is such a great element of godly character because it's a daily thing. See, gifts will manifest here and there as needed for the moment. Gifts are great but they can come and go and are available on occasion. Yet excellence is continual. It's a superb, high quality, supreme, matchless, exemplary, and exceptional way of life. This manifests in *who you are* and in *what you do,* from the way you conduct ministry to the way you care for your home. Unfortunately, this attribute is often neglected or forgotten. Yet we cannot afford to forget that God the Father, God the Son, and God the Holy Ghost are in complete excellent harmony in their functions and manifestations.

Jesus prayed, "Your kingdom come. Your will be done on earth as it is in heaven" (Matthew 6:10). Consider the context of this prayer. He is praying this over a fallen earth. Too often, we think minor upgrades and temporary fixes are excellence, when in reality heaven coming and manifesting in our midst is true excellence. If God dwells in excellence we have to consider His heavenly domain. In heaven there are 12 gates made of one solid piece of pearl and there are streets of gold. I've had the incredible honor of being caught up in heavenly visitations and visions, and I can tell you firsthand, when you see heaven—you will not come back with a poverty mentality. You won't embrace a spirit of lack when you see God's domain.

To give you a quick anecdote to galvanize this, I was waiting on the Lord one day and saw a vision of the pearly gates in heaven. It was one solid piece of pearl with an archtop that slid open to let people in. Because of industry experience, I have an eye for construction and quite a bit of experience in custom homes and I can tell you one of the more expensive features a home can have is arch-topped windows and doors. If clients needed to cut costs, we could do so easily by squaring off these elements. The gates of pearl are not squared off. Not only that but putting windows and doors on hinges was always a cheaper option, whereas anything that slides needs special tracks and more work. They are small details but recognizing them helped me to see just how excellent God is in all that He does.

Now, I don't want you to feel like in order to be excellent you need to blow your budget on the fanciest materials and decadent spaces. But what I am saying is that our personalities, outlooks, expressions, ministries, work, families and domains must reflect the excellence that is God Himself. Let's be real, hell is a place of dysfunction, filth, disorder and chaos. Even when you look at geography, where sin has saturated an area, the very look of hell is evident. Yet where God saturates an area, excellence is commonplace.

I've seen ministers and ministries that are heavily anointed and infatuated with Jesus yet lacking a spirit of excellence. Don't get me wrong, excellence is not the sole ingredient in the recipe of success. Yet without excellence, the recipe is incomplete.

For example, you could go into a meeting where the anointing is strong, gifts are flowing, people are falling out under the power of God, the preaching is on-point, yet the sanctuary is a mess. The carpet is torn up. The ushers are in disarray. Light bulbs are missing. The resource area is chaotic. You get the picture. Excellence obviously is not the *be all, end all* of life and ministry, but without it—people notice its absence. One of the best examples of people beholding excellence is found in the Queen of Sheba's visit to Solomon's temple:

> "And when the queen of Sheba had seen all the wisdom of Solomon, the house that he had built the food on his table, the seating of his servants, the service of his waiters and their apparel, his cupbearers, and his entryway by which he went up to the house of the Lord, there was no more spirit in her. Then she said to the king: 'It was a true report which I heard in my own land about your words and your wisdom. However I did not believe the words until I came and saw with my own eyes; and indeed the half was not told me. Your wisdom and prosperity exceed the fame of which I heard.'" (1 Kings 10:4-7)

She was so undone by the beauty and excellence of Solomon's temple that she became breathless. She hadn't seen anything like it. Solomon had funding and blueprints from David's legacy, and an unmatched wisdom and excellence that caused him to build something that was a testimony to the excellence of God. In fact, the queen was so inspired that she gave a massive offering when she saw this. Excellence gave Solomon favor with the leaders of the nations.

Commit yourself to walk in a spirit of excellence in every

area of life. Leave nothing unchecked. I know that some people are more detail oriented than others, and that's okay. However, we all could use a boost in excellence to care about the details and exude the beauty of God in all areas.

25

FOREVER FAITHFUL

"A faithful man will abound with blessings..." (Proverbs 28:20)

FAITHFUL MEANS *STEADFASTNESS, firmness, loyalty, consistency, true, devoted, unswerving, committed, dependable, reliable, trustworthy.* True faithfulness in God can be hard to find. Yet it is the fabric of our faith. Every other element of relationship with Jesus rides on faithfulness. He Himself is ever faithful, in fact, He is described this way in Revelation, "Now I saw heaven opened, and behold, a white horse. And He who sat on him was called Faithful and True, and in righteousness He judges and makes war" (Revelation 19:11). Naturally, if Christ exudes it, we are called to as well.

"His lord said to him, 'Well done, good and faithful servant; you were faithful over a few things, I will make you ruler over many things. Enter into the joy of your lord.'" (Matthew 25:21)

Notice, Jesus did not say, "Well done my good and talented servant," or "well done my good and anointed servant," but instead He used the word *faithful*. Paul said, "Moreover it is required in stewards that one be found faithful" (1 Corinthians 4:2). In my own life in ministry or even in working as a contractor prior to ministry, I've given little tasks and resources to people in order to gage their faithfulness. Obviously, it's unwise to give much to one who hasn't been found faithful or hasn't proven their faithfulness. It's a biblical principle and God places a premium on it. The Bible commands us, "Never let loyalty and kindness leave you!" (Proverbs 3:3 NLT). Notice, *kindness*, which we touched on earlier, and *loyalty* are tied together. Each of the attributes described in this book correlate in some way, shape or form.

Loyalty is often forsaken when a temporary opportunity arises. As a result we lose the real opportunity that God had for us. That real opportunity would have catapulted us into our destinies. Jesus instructed us to be faithful over the little and as a result we will be made a ruler over much (see Luke 16:10). Most people want to be ruler over much but bypass the little. It doesn't work that way. When we attempt to bypass faithfulness with the little, we short-circuit the process and end up with less than little.

It all comes back to this question: *what did God say?* When you have a Word from Him, you cling to it. Any door that opens that doesn't agree with His will, you refuse to walk through by remaining in faithfulness. Some get fooled because they're led by open doors. Yet we aren't to be led by open doors. We are led by the will and Spirit of God.

Sometimes even a *good* door opens, yet if you walk through it, you'd be sacrificing faithfulness. To give you a quick example, a person might be called as an itinerant speaker. Then suddenly they are offered a position as a pastor of a great church. It's an open door and a great setting. It isn't a carnal thing. It's not a fleshly temptation. Yet when God is not giving a green light, jumping into it would be a sacrifice of faithfulness.

So often we get busy jumping into ventures and pathways that God didn't ordain. Even in these trivial pursuits we can see fruit, salvations, healings and so forth, because God's word never returns void. Yet it still isn't the optimal place of fulfilment for us. Stick yourself to the will of God. Be glued to His instructions.

Now, seasons can shift, anointings can lift, and destiny can be redirected. God may have called you to live in Los Angeles a decade ago yet now He is calling you to Seattle. We can pivot in the Spirit. But the quintessential call is to cling to His voice and leading, regardless of circumstances and trivial opportunities.

See, everyone wants to show up when the task seems prominent, noteworthy, and likely to garner applause. Yet true faithfulness will do far more than what's applauded by the public. It will do the tasks in the trenches that no one sees for the sole purpose of honoring the Lord in a heart of faithfulness. There's plenty of fake, shallow, "scratch my back and I'll scratch yours" mentalities floating in our culture. Yet faithfulness inspires us to do good, not merely when there is a return heading our way but when no reward seems to be evident.

26

INTERNAL INTEGRITY

"The integrity of the upright guides them, but the unfaithful are destroyed by their duplicity." (Proverbs 11:3 NIV)

NOTICE, the opposite of integrity is to live in *duplicity*. That word duplicity means to have double-dealings. It's to split attention between good and evil. The enemy would like for you to be spread thin with divided attention. Yet we have an integrous, single-eyed call to Jesus. You can't have division in your soul. When you look at the word division it's di-vision meaning two-visions. It's a split in focus that can cost you greatly.

To be integrous is to be upright, innocent, blameless, moral, noble, honorable, and with virtue. It's not serving the Lord while doing the devil's bidding on the side. The mere definition of integrity sounds like stability, and like someone you'd want to be around. "Whoever walks in integrity walks securely, but whoever takes crooked paths will be found out" (Proverbs 10:9 NIV). There is a blessing found in integrity. Why? Because integrity can be trusted. Integrity will do the right thing regardless of whether or not there is a crowd. It's easy to do good when applause awaits you. But integrity works for the approval of one, namely Jesus Himself.

> "I know that you are pleased with me, for my enemy does not triumph over me. Because of my integrity you uphold me and set me in your presence forever." (Psalm 41:11-12 NIV)

David understood the value of integrity toward God. The byproduct of that was victory over the enemy, being upheld by God, and lastly *and most importantly,* that he would be set up in God's presence forever. Integrity elevates you to glory. David also said, "May integrity and uprightness protect me" (Psalm 25:21 NIV). Think of integrity like salt. It's a preservative in our lives.

The interesting thing about integrity is that you have the chance to flesh this out in the little things and the big things. Integrity wants to show up in the small decisions that no one sees and in the big ones that are public. Small compromises work against integrity. Yet God wants to use us as standard bearers for what character looks like in this world. This means when you're at the grocery store, you put the baskets and carts back where they belong when you're done. If a cashier hands you more money than they should have, don't pocket it. When you do there's a chance that the employee will be paying for that error out of their own paycheck. Do the right thing and hand it back.

Integrity doesn't take advantage of situations, big or small. Integrity remains on the straight and narrow at all times. Galatians teaches that you reap what you sow. If integrity does not work in the small things it doesn't work in the big things either. As Jesus said, if you aren't faithful with the small you won't be faithful with the big. You could swap out the word *faithful* with the word *integrity* and you would not be doing the scripture injustice. "He who has integrity with the small things will have integrity in the big things."

Learn from the examples of men like Enoch, Job, Noah and other patriarchs. They walked with God faithfully. It doesn't mean that they were spotless, yet they exemplified integrity and faithfulness. Esther, Hannah, the woman of Tekoa, Mary and other ladies in Scripture embodied these attributes in remarkable ways. Paul said, "Now all these things happened to them as examples, and they were written for our admonition, upon whom the ends of the ages have come" (1 Corinthians 10:11). Our call is to examine these figures and duplicate what they did right, while avoiding what they got wrong.

Integrity ought to be a marker in our lives by which people can identify us. Many things come and go, yet integrity and godly character are to be the steadfast anchor, keeping our spirits, souls, and bodies in alignment with heaven.

27

CONCLUSIVE THOUGHTS

THE VARIED ELEMENTS of character that we touched on throughout this book are by no means exhaustive. We could write volumes and volumes of books on dozens, if not, hundreds of other aspects of godly character. Yet the fundamental truth is this: intimacy with Jesus will birth in you a desire to put on love and to put off anything that doesn't look like love.

Love is the origin of any and all character traits that are worthwhile in our lives. My prayer is that this book has given you a deeper and fresher understanding of the character of God and the character we are called to emulate. There are many gifted, anointed, talented and skilled people in the world, and we are all for this. Yet in our celebration of these things, let us not forget that godly character is the actual cornerstone that allows these ancillary items to rest securely in our lives.

PRAYER FOR CHARACTER

Father, I pray for each precious saint reading this book. I hold them before You and ask that You would grant to them a supernatural grace to begin to build new levels of character. In the same way that one might remodel and add onto a house, I pray You would remodel us and add onto us. We may have come a long way, but there is so much more purity, holiness and transformation available. Thank You, for being the architect of our lives both in precept and in example, in Jesus name, amen.

ABOUT THE AUTHOR

BRIAN GUERIN is the founding president of Bridal Glory International. He graduated from the Brownsville School of Ministry/F.I.R.E. in 2001, and now travels throughout the U.S. and the world teaching and preaching the gospel of the Lord Jesus Christ. Brian has appeared on T.B.N. and GOD-TV and currently hosts his own broadcasting channel on YouTube. He also authored two previously released books, *Modern Day Mysticism* and *God of Wonders*. His main passion and emphasis in life is to draw the Bride of Christ into greater intimacy with the Bridegroom Himself-Jesus Christ, leading to the maturity of the Bride and the culmination of His glorious return. Brian also enjoys bringing great emphasis and depth to the art of hearing the voice of God through dreams, visions, signs, and wonders.

VISIT BRIDAL GLORY ON THE WEB & SOCIAL:
WWW.BRIDALGLORY.COM

SOCIAL: @BRIDALGLORY

FREE EXCERTP FROM
Angelic Hosts

AVAILABLE AT
amazon

INTRODUCTION

The letter alone kills but the Spirit gives life. I've always been one who can't merely read the Word, I've got to experience the Word. What is Christianity if not *experiential*? My aim with this book is simple: to raise expectations for encounters, namely *angelic activity* in your own life. This biblically dominant force is often overlooked in our day to day routines. I pray that by and through these chapters, you will find yourself growing with expectation to partner with God's angelic realm.

Prior to producing this material, I had a dream in which a doctor approached a person who was struggling with their eyesight. I sensed that the doctor represented the angelic. In this dream the patient didn't actually realize that they had a problem with their eyes, yet the doctor approached, inspected, and assisted in opening the patient's eyes to be able to see clearly. I knew that this represented angelic aid in opening spiritual eyes.

Like in the dream, we often aren't able to recognize our own blindness. We don't recognize *blind spots* because they are just that...blind spots. We don't have the capacity to measure our visual capability in the spirit. We must have our eyes opened to be able to see the unseen with 20/20 vision. Dreams, visions, and trances are ever available, yet an opening of the eyes is required. I pray that through this book, you'll step into a 20/20 awakening, as it were—that you would *see* and *know* that which is occurring in the spirit realm around you. May angelic aid be available to aid, assist and encounter you as you step forward in your journey!

CHAPTER ONE
NECESSITY AND EXPECTANCY

Angels are mentioned over 270 times in Scripture. Far too often, we are influenced by a religious spirit, quite frankly, and we are talked out of our inheritance which includes partnership with the angelic. This is not the time nor the season to be walking in 30% or 40% of God's kingdom. It is time that we walk in 100% of the kingdom of God and His angelic resources. It is time to fire on all cylinders. We see darkness covering the earth in these days, as the Bible speaks of, but at the same time—we see the glory of God covering the world as well. When the world makes a move, God is already several steps ahead. It is the blessed benefit of serving an omniscient Creator! Jesus said, "Greater works you will do..." (see John 14:12)

Some rebut with, "Yeah, but He was only talking about quantity because He was only doing ministry for three years." No, it is both quantity and quality. Why? Because it is Him doing it to begin with! When Christ promised us greater works, He wasn't removing Himself from the equation. He was essentially saying, "I'll be doing greater works through you." Jesus' garment was touched and a woman was healed. Decades later, Paul had sweaty work rags taken from him and placed on the demon possessed and they were healed. Do you see the upgrade? Greater works were already beginning in the record of Acts and greater works are still continuing to this day. Besides, whether it was a pinky being healed or someone walking out of a wheelchair, it's all Jesus anyway.

A religious spirit will attempt to talk you out of these things. A religious spirit will convince you that you'll be easily deceived when you begin tapping into miracles, healings and the angelic realm. Yet, the Bible is littered with authentic angelic encounters, sent from God, and God wasn't in paranoia regarding His people and their relationship to angels.

Anytime that I've encountered angels in my life, I've never been drawn to worship them or found myself distracted from Christ. In fact, God-sent angels always pull you toward Jesus. They don't want the attention. Folks often mean well when they attempt to warn us of deception. Yet despite being well meaning, many people are hindering others from stepping into the fulness of what God has. Someone might begin to speak about sensing an angel in their midst and a well meaning brother says, "Well, you better be careful of deception...even the elect can be deceived." Then suddenly that person withdraws from their experience, shuts down sensitivity to angels and lives in a fear of deception. This isn't God's best.

The Lord Jesus is inexhaustible. His Kingdom, His realms, His glory, graces, resources, angel armies, clouds of witnesses, signs and wonders, and so forth are absolutely inexhaustible. To box God into a theological framework that doesn't match up with Scripture is to limit our potential in experiencing and walking in the fullness of the Kingdom.

Much of the religious thinking regarding angels stems from a fear of deception. The problem is, that which you fear you ultimately become subject to. If you fear it, you will eventually be mastered by it. Therefore, when you are fearful and intimidated by the thought of deception, it is very, very easy to step into deception itself. Many spouting, "Don't be deceived," are actually deceived themselves while walking in 1% of the Kingdom when they're called to 100% of the Kingdom. Satan loves to limit access to these things by twisting pet Scriptures to hinder our vision.

Some of you reading this might have limited-to-no experience of angels in your life. Others might have seen sporadic glimpses of angels at work in your midst. Regardless of where you are with it, God wants to release constant availability to you in this realm. It's what we see in Scripture and it's what is intended for our lives. As we grow and learn in these areas, we experience enlightenment and understanding. As our enlightenment and understanding grows, we increase in faith and expectancy and the encounters only increase as a result. Thus we find ourselves in a divine cycle of visitation and habitation concerning angels.

ANGELIC ATTRIBUTES

> "Are they (angels) not all ministering spirits sent out to serve for the sake of those who are to inherit salvation?"
> (Hebrews 1:14 emphasis added)

We can spot from the text that angels are spirits. While they might manifest looking like people at times, they are not people. They come from an eternal realm and exist outside of time. From this passage we also see that they are ministers. They are servants. They love to do the will of God. Not only that, but they have a specific focus on ministry to those who will inherit salvation and those who have inherited salvation. To those not walking in the Kingdom, angelic activity can be minimal or even nonexistent.

Sometimes in life, we find ourselves experiencing duplicity and multiplicity in our interests, affections and paths. Perhaps for a season you find yourself straying from the sole focus of your calling or dabbling in other things that God hasn't ordained. Unlike us, angels are singularly focused in their purpose and intent. The angels assigned to you have one job: assist you in your calling. They are continually assisting, serving and ministering to you with the ultimate goal of enabling you to walk out the fullness of your destiny. The blueprint we see in Scripture is the angelic encountering great generals like Jacob, Paul, Peter, Mary, Daniel, Moses, Joshua, Gideon and others. Again, if these men and women who went about great exploits for God and had need of an angelic visitation, how much more could we use them today? In fact the Word describes Christ encountering angels in this way:

> "Jesus said to him, 'Again it is written, 'You shall not put the Lord your God to the test.'" Again, the devil took him to a very high mountain and showed him all the kingdoms

of the world and their glory. And He said to him, 'All these I will give you, if you will fall down and worship me.' Then Jesus said to him, 'Be gone, Satan! For it is written, "You shall worship the Lord your God and Him only shall you serve.' Then the devil left him, and behold, angels came and were ministering to him.'" (Matthew 4:7-11)

If the perfect, spotless Son of God in the flesh needed angelic support, how much more do we need it as well? He is the highest standard. He is the perfect model of what life in a physical body should look like here on earth. Don't miss these quick passages on angelic help. You can't afford to miss out on the assistance that Christ Himself needed in the earth.

"Yet You have made him a little lower than the heavenly beings and crowned him with glory and honor. You have given him dominion over the works of your hands; You have put all things under his feet." (Psalm 8:5-6)

The phrase heavenly beings in this passage, of course, refers to angels. This passage reveals that there is a ranking and an order among created beings. As of now, we sit slightly below angels in our rank. A New Testament passage reflects this same passage:

"What is man, that you are mindful of him, or the son of man, that you care for him? You made him for a little while lower than the angels; you have crowned him with glory and honor, putting everything in subjection under his feet." (Hebrews 2:6-8)

Notice, angels are superior currently. Some speculate that there will be a day when that shifts as the Scripture says, "Beloved, we are God's children now, and what we will be has not yet appeared; but we know that when He appears we shall be like Him, because we shall see Him as He is" (1 John 3:2 emphasis added). Also, Paul points out, "Do you not know that we are to judge angels?" (1 Corinthians 6:3)

Why does this matter? Because for the time being, we find ourselves in a lower rank than angels, as a result, their activity isn't to be overlooked, neglected or scoffed at. There is a natural honor that flows upward when we understand these things. Whether it was Peter being freed from jail by an angel or an angel speaking out of the burning bush—biblical figures needed this presence and so do we. Angels carry the voice of the Lord and provide commissionings and sendings. They sometimes communicate in parables and sometimes provide insight and revelation. Essentially, an angel is like a microphone in the hand of God, amplifying the Lord's voice to you personally in a variety of ways. As this book unfolds, we'll target several of these functions. These realities and characteristics ought to stir faith and expectancy within you. They should highlight and exemplify our need for more.

"Jacob left Beersheba and went towards Haran. And he came to a certain place and stayed there that night, because the sun had set. Taking one of the stones of the place, he put it under his head and lay down in that place to sleep." (Genesis 28:10-11)

Notice, Jacob came to a certain place, the Bible says. God loves places. He loves specific spots and regions to be markers for glory. As you journey with Jesus you'll find that particular regions, places, perhaps spots in your home and so forth become portals, openings and gateways for heaven and the angelic. Let's continue:

"And he dreamed, and behold, there was a ladder set up on the earth, and the top of it reached to heaven. And behold, the angels of God were ascending and descending on it!" (Genesis 28:12)

This is absolutely a flagship set of Scriptures on the subject of angels. The angels in this passage first ascended up to heaven. After that, what did they do? They descended to the earth! Notice the motion and path of travel for angels. They relocate back and forth between the presence of God and the earth. Angels are not omnipresent. They cannot be everywhere at once, like God can. However, because they exist in the spirit-world, they are able to transport anywhere in the earth in the blink of an eye. They are limited to one space in time but they aren't limited in their ability to get there quickly. Humans are bound by natural laws of physics and gravity. Angels are not subject to such things. Many people think that angels merely exist in the heavens.

However, as we've seen—they are quite busy in the earth and in their ministry. The passage goes on to say:

> "And behold, the Lord stood above it and said, 'I am the Lord, the God of Abraham your father and the God of Isaac. The land on which you lie I will give to you and to your offspring. Your offspring shall be like the dust of the earth, and you shall spread abroad to the west and to the east and to the north and to the south, and in you and your offspring shall all the families of the earth be blessed. Behold, I am with you and will keep you wherever you go, and will bring you back to this land. For I will not leave you until I have done what I have promised you.'" (Genesis 28:13-15)

What we see in this declaration is the Lord gives a blessing, a commissioning, and a promise given. All of them are tied into angelic encounters. Many either see the ladder alone with angels or see the blessing which God gave afterward. However, they are both linked. God is at the top of the ladder providing the commissioning, promise and blessing. We are on the receiving end at the bottom of the ladder. And angels are running up and down on the ladder communicating and assisting in fulfilling the commissions and promises God gave to us.

We are much more fluid, effective and useful in the earth when we align ourselves to these realities. It isn't complicated. In fact, it is the opposite of complicated. Angelic help makes things easier. You might say, "Where does the Holy

Spirit work in all of this?" He is the general of the angelic realm in the earth! It is the protocol of heaven. I love it all, because it's all from Jesus! These things are found in Him and working through Him.

Angels are a means to an end. They are not an end in themselves. I like to use this example: imagine that God is a Gardener who commissions you to help Him plant and cultivate a piece of ground. He has a garden with soil, seeds, water, and sunshine to assist in the process. In order to grow plants, you need to watch the weather, plant at the appropriate time, till the soil, work the ground, use a watering can, and monitor the growth. It would be odd to simply focus on the Gardener and consider the till, the rake, and the watering can distractions, wouldn't it? Yet so many people do this with the angelic realm.

The angelic is a mere tool used to get the job done. Yet so many are ignoring the tools and just expecting the Gardner to do it all. Allow God to open up your awareness of His tool kit in your life. Embrace your need for this realm and consider the necessity of angels in your present circumstances. In this, you'll posture yourself properly and you will become an attractant to these heavenly beings.

*ENTIRE BOOK CAN BE PURCHASED IN **PAPERBACK** AND **EBOOK** FORMATS ON **AMAZON.COM**